DYSLEXIA

The Problem of Reading

by

Joy Pollock

Published by and obtainable from
The Helen Arkell Dyslexia Centre,
14 Crondace Road, London SW6 4BB
© February, 1976
ISBN 0 9503626 7 0

This series includes the following titles:

Page Layouts Brian Roll
Printed by The Fairway Press Ltd.

Introduction

Dyslexia is often considered to be solely a reading disability, or backwardness in reading, and as such to be part of a continuum of reading abilities from the very poorest to the most proficient. This is not so; it has been found that a cluster of disabilities is usually present together with the reading disability.[1] Remedial tuition, therefore, needs to cover all aspects of the problem and should vary from that given to other children in remedial groups. In these groups there may well be immigrant children who will need to be taught a new vocabulary, quite probably the Roman letters and English syntax, and then the art of reading and spelling the English language. Others may have changed school many times and been exposed to a variety of methods which together have done more to confuse than enlighten them. Some may have had inexperienced teachers. Others may have a hearing loss and be unaware of certain sounds, and yet others may have poor eyesight and be unable to see clearly the words in front of them. Some may be emotionally disturbed, and there are those whose intelligence is limited and as a consequence they will learn at a rather slower rate than their peers anyway. And then, finally, there may be one or two dyslexics in the group—children who perhaps are highly intelligent, whose eyesight and hearing is good, who have been to good schools where experienced teachers in small classes have helped them all they can, and yet these children fail to read adequately, or even at all. Eventually they may join the numbers of illiterate adults and many try to hide their secret with shame for the rest of their lives.

This specific problem with reading and spelling, and the related problems of sequencing and orientation, has been termed 'dyslexia'—derived from the Greek signifying 'difficulty with words'. Analysis of the disability will reveal details such as poor visual perception, poor auditory perception, problems of sequencing and orientation. It is the dyslexic's misfortune that our present educational system is based on skills which are his weaknesses. No matter how intelligent he is, no matter how good he is at other things, unless he can read and write with average fluency, he will be unable to get very far in acquiring the qualifications which indicate a degree of scholastic success so neccessary nowadays to future employment.

[1] See *Dyslexia: A Dyslexic's Eye-View*, by Helen Arkell.

1

This ability to read, and the related skill of writing (which includes spelling) has long been equated with intelligence and education. It is a traditional attitude that has been handed down through the centuries—people able to acquire knowledge through books are intelligent, and those who cannot are stupid and only fit for menial jobs.

In fact there is no reason for equating the ability to read with intelligence any more than there is the ability to draw. Some people are able to read with ease, and avidly sift knowledge from one book after another. Others cannot do this. If we had to act or sing our way through school there would be a different group of children in the remedial section—and no doubt a different group of teachers in charge too! Just as a person may be intelligent but not necessarily musical, so may a person be intelligent but unable to read.

During the course of this century, as schooling has become universal in western countries, it has been more noticeable that there is a group of children who, 'despite conventional classroom experience, fail to attain the language skills of reading, writing and spelling commensurate with their intellectual abilities.'[1] Dr. Margaret Newton asserts that these children have a good spatial ability, and many have neither right nor left cerebral dominance, but have a tendency to ambilaterality.

Each person is individual. If the reason for someone's inability to sing in tune, for instance, were analysed it might well be found to stem from poor auditory perception, poor auditory retention and an inability to concentrate on musical notes for longer than a very limited time. But this is not usually gone into because only people with a natural ability for music delight in singing or playing an instrument. Despite the fact that there must be a reason for people not being in the least musical, it is not thought of as an abnormality in any way, and certainly not related to intelligence. Perhaps this is due to this particular talent not being vital to success in our present educational system, as are reading and writing.

In the same way there are physiological reasons for dyslexia, but one must stand back and see this inability to cope with written symbols—whether one accepts the reason to be due to a neurological deficiency or not—in the same light as these other disabilities. Dyslexics are not abnormal. It is convenient to give a name to this specific disability, as it is to others.

In our present society a lot of communication between people is written. Letters, books, essays, notes, as well as the inevitable forms to be filled in, all require an ability to read and write. This results in dyslexics feeling very inadequate. This feeling of inadequacy is increased by the traditional attitude towards literacy. Often the automatic reaction of teachers and peers alike to this disability is that the person in question must be either stupid or lazy.

---

[1]One of two definitions recommended by The Research Group on Developmental Dyslexia of the World Federation of Neurology in 1968.

Inevitably his confidence is eroded and even the most intelligent dyslexic has a sneaking feeling that these labels may be correct.

Some people argue that to give this problem a name makes an individual feel at an even greater disadvantage than if a term such as 'slow reader' were used. The medical profession has long recognised the therapeutic benefit of terminology. If a child at school is unable to read when his friends appear to be mastering the art with comparative ease, he will be just as anxious as a person who has a continual pain and has no idea what the matter is. Just as the latter will feel a sense of relief when told what his illness is and given a course of treatment, so does the dyslexic when he knows why he is failing and is given the necessary remedial teaching. Children and adults coming to our Centres for their first lesson are told what their problem is. It is discussed in a sympathetic, but straightforward, way. Pupils then realise that they will have to work very hard. Once they understand the situation feelings of relief and determination supplant those of frustration and bewilderment.

Society's attitude towards illiteracy does untold damage. Without stopping to think of the effect, people tend to adopt a superior and scornful attitude to anyone who cannot read. If a person is physically unable to read, because of poor eyesight or because he has left his spectacles behind, it is understood immediately. But the dyslexic's predicament has no obvious physical causes and is consequently seldom understood.

It is no wonder therefore that a dyslexic feels he must cover up his disability. This may start quite early in school when, as a small child, he may get help from a more successful friend when his turn for reading comes up. As he continues through school his subterfuges may become more complex—truancy, sickness (often very real and the result of acute anxiety), 'forgetting' books, etc.—and in adulthood he may be known to carry an empty spectacle-case—"Oh, I have left my specs. behind!"—or suddenly have 'headaches' at awkward moments. In these enlightened times in education it is amazing how many children manage to get through their school-days without being able to read, or only able to do so inadequately.

Later in life they become quite ingenious at finding ways and means of covering up dyslexia. A married man, aged 35, once came for reading lessons. He said that he had been married for two years before his wife found out that he could not read, and no one at work knew of his disability. Despite his handicap he had been earning a high salary—in fact, twice the average teacher's salary! On the other hand, he had been referred for treatment by the court. It was felt that had he been able to read he might have avoided being the dupe of 'friends' in a conviction for stealing turkeys.

Such a person lives an anxious existence, constantly in fear of his illiteracy being found out. Not only does he feel that his relationships with other people are dishonest, but also that he is living out a lie and not being honest with himself either. He is often wary of forming close relationships and his life lacks stability. Parties can become an anathema and an otherwise sociable person may find himself beating a hasty retreat as soon as there are signs of 'danger'. "Let's play scrabble!", or some party-game involving reading or spelling, will often force a dyslexic to find an excuse to scurry back home.

Recently a family-man pointed out that ten years ago he could get a job after a discussion with a prospective employer. Now, even for the humblest of jobs, forms have to be filled in and paper qualifications are required. He considered himself to be a particularly careful driver. He knew, however, that if he were involved in an accident he would be required to supply details in writing—an embarrassing situation which he wanted to avoid at all costs. He applied for a job as a bus driver, but felt he must be honest about his predicament and so he explained that he could not read. He was immediately turned down because of the reading involved (time-tables, street names, etc.). No **help** was offered. After periods of depression and attempted suicide he eventually found his way to the Dyslexia Centre, and suitable remedial treatment was arranged for him. He turns up regularly for his lessons and is getting enormous satisfaction from learning to read. He is also gaining in self-respect, and family relationships are improving.

Many dyslexics drift from job to job; as soon as they are put in a position where they have to read or fill in forms their position becomes unbearable and leaving becomes an escape. Promotion may entail written work, so even advancement can be a worry. Some are in rather menial work, despite high intelligence. They tend to feel inadequate, uncertain and on the defensive. Their lives may lack any plan because they are never quite sure what is available, as this entails reading. They are in a similar position to people who have to rely on the social services for information and help in sorting out their problems. They are not aware of the adverts in the papers, or the situations vacant. And in any case what possible interpretation could be given to abbreviations, such as 'PSV drivers reqd.', 'Autos inc. B.S.A. Nos. 30A & 38' or 'S/C villas or aparts., £25 p.w. max.'? Dyslexics may live impulsively. They may hear that a job is free, or of a play that is on, and instead of weighing the possibility of one vacant job against another or selecting one entertainment from the rest, their lives are directed by these chance bits of information. They are dependent on other people for knowledge, picking up information from television or the discussions of people around them, rather than the printed word. The dependence on others for knowledge can leave a feeling of deep resentment.

However, the problem of dyslexia should not be considered to be one of complete illiteracy any more than it should be thought of as solely a reading problem. There are of course many dyslexics, both children and adults, who can barely read their names. At the other end of the dyslexic scale there are people who have had a certain amount of difficulty in learning to read, but whose intelligence is good enough to get the general sense out of what they are reading (despite any mis-readings). There are also those whose dyslexia is mild enough for them only to have a limited problem anyway. As children they usually manage to 'get by' at school, but many of them run into difficulties when doing further training requiring written examinations. Some may manage to do 'A' levels and get to University, but reading may still be a laborious task and the number of books on a syllabus often poses a big problem. It is every bit as important that these people should have remedial tuition and realise their full potential ability as those who cannot read at all.

So we in the remedial field have before us the vast and varied task of trying to remedy the difficulties that children and adults have in interpreting written symbols. From the completely illiterate who cannot recall the shapes and sounds of letters to the student who is handicapped by being a slow and faulty reader, expert remedial tuition is a vital necessity.

Some indications of the problem

A dyslexic's difficulty in learning to read is due to poor perception of symbols. Perception is the ability to understand through the senses. Letters are symbols for sounds in language. The dyslexic's disability lies in the recognition and recall of letters (visual perception) and in giving the correct sounds to letters and digraphs (auditory perception). Added to this there is the need to get the letters in the correct order when reading a word (often known as 'sequencing'), and letters have to face a particular way (known as 'orientation'); these present further problems.[1]

Poor Visual Perception

Visual perception is the ability to see shapes and understand what they represent—in other words, to recognise and interpret symbols. Poor visual perception has nothing to do with bad eyesight. Dyslexics have difficulty in recalling the shapes of letters, and this is needed for writing and spelling; they also have difficulty in recognising letters, which is a necessity for reading. For instance, one dyslexic boy, when asked to name a capital 'B' which was written on the blackboard, thought it was a pair of spectacles; he had just not seen it as a letter at all.

Not only is there difficulty in recognising an individual letter, but also a group of letters, a syllable or a whole word. Most people take mental photographs of words they see, and then reproduce the image in their mind's eye when they want to write a particular word, or recognise it when they come to read it. Some dyslexics are able to recognise word-pictures when they see them again, but have difficulty in recalling words when writing. These are the people whose reading is good, but whose spelling is bad. If the visual recall is weak, then the mental picture of the word is blurred, or even non-existent. We have all experienced instances where holiday photographs have failed to come out, or are badly exposed, and it is as though this is constantly happening with the dyslexic and mental photographs of words. Consequently he has to rely on relating sounds to letters, blending the sounds into words in the hope that he will recognise them that way, and that the meaning of the text

[1]Yet another problem may be the association of meaning with the written word.

will then become apparent. One often notices that a dyslexic painstakingly builds up a word on one line, and even if the word is repeated on the following line he looks at it as though he has never seen it before and has to sound out the letters all over again. For the fluent reader the ability to retain the visual image of words is essential. As a large percentage of people have this ability the look-and-say method of teaching reading has had much success; but, because people with very poor visual perception could not learn by this method and failed badly, the approach has also done much to highlight the problem of the dyslexic. With poor visual perception there must be a phonic approach to reading.

Poor Auditory Perception

Auditory perception is the ability to hear sounds and understand what they represent. Poor auditory perception is not related to a loss of hearing. Although a dyslexic may be able to hear a pin drop, he could be unable to discriminate between certain letter-sounds, such as 'e' and 'i', or 's' and 'sh', and 'm' and 'n'. There may be confusion between voiced and voiceless sounds and the relevant letters, like 'd' and 't', 'b' and 'p', and 'g' and 'k'. With language, sounds have to be recognised and linked to letters and words, and their meanings.

Usually dyslexics have poor auditory perception as well as poor visual perception. Where auditory perception is poor, the letter-sounds are only learnt with great difficulty, and even when this has been achieved there is a problem with blending them and sequencing them correctly. Dyslexics also find it particularly difficult to isolate sounds within a word. They cannot readily add a letter-sound to a word, such as 'an'—'v-an' or 'an-d'; or omit a letter-sound, as in 'trip'—'rip' or 'tip'. Having built up a word like 'van', if the 'v' is replaced by a 'p', for instance, they cannot see or hear that they now have 'pan'. If an 'l' is inserted after 'p' they have great difficulty in arriving at the word 'plan'. Each word has to be laboriously sounded out and blended. The dyslexic is slow to understand word families.

These children with poor auditory perception may have difficulty in rhyming words. A 15-year-old girl was asked for words rhyming with 'stick' and gave "whip, lip, keep and wheat". Dyslexics also find it difficult to divide words up into syllables because they are unaware of the rhythm of a word. They are continually mispronouncing words, like "renember", "geogaphry", "emeny" and "intranfy"—usual enough in 5-6 year olds, but, when these are continually used by 10 and 12 year olds, teachers may find that this is linked to a reading problem. More colourful mispronunciations that have been produced by dyslexic pupils have been "chapular" for 'bachelor' and "sgabetti" for 'spaghetti'. One boy of eight told an American visitor that he could hear her "accident" (accent) and, when playing at soldiers, was heard shouting "Bang! Bang! Bang! You're deadicated!" A girl of almost 13 opened a copy of *Jane Eyre* and remarked: "This is a different virgin" (version). Many people make mistakes of this kind occasionally when they are tired, but with dyslexics they are cropping up all the time and often only noticed in the quiet of a one-to-one relationship.

People with poor auditory perception lack the rhythm of language. They may not be able to tap out a rhythm or clap in time. Foreign languages usually cause them difficulty. Learning poetry by heart is an anathema to most of them. They often put the wrong emphasis on syllables of words, and when reading may make several attempts at a multisyllabic word before getting it correct. By that time the meaning of the word is often lost, and the meaning of the sentence too. A girl of 12, and of good intelligence, read for 'stable-man', "stallible", then "stillable", and then "stable". For 'neglect' she read "necklet . . ." and then "necklace of his horse". In other words a dyslexic fails to take in the whole word, notes certain details, and then may guess the rest—often wrongly!

Sequencing

The sequencing problem occurs because the dyslexic does not tackle words consistently from left to right. Dyslexics have similar problems in Arabic or Chinese, no matter from what direction it is customary to read. One reads with the mind; sight is one of the senses through which the information is transferred. (Braille readers use the sense of touch.) Poor directional attack on words has nothing to do with eyesight or with muscular movements of the eyes; it is due to poor reading ability and is not the cause of it.[1] Each word has its own characteristic shape, and certain letter-combinations stand out. These give the reader a clue to that word. If words are read in context the sense of the text confirms (or rejects) the correct reading of each word. Most dyslexics cannot perceive the whole word without considerable training.[2] It is possible that they glance across it from left to right, do not take it in, and then go back from right to left, and as a result read, for instance, "was" for "saw", or "on" for "no", which are complete reversals; or partially reverse words such as "left" for "felt" or "being" for "begin"; or transpose letters, like "indeed" for "hidden" or "noise" for "onions". They may read words and phrases more than once, or omit them altogether. Syllables are sometimes added, as in "subtitle" for "subtle", or omitted as in "future" for "furniture" and "while" for "whistle". A line of text is often missed out—even when a

[1]See *The Dyslexic Child,* by Macdonald Critchley, published by Heinemann, page 58: "Faulty eye-movements must be regarded as the outcome of a difficulty in reading, and not its cause."
[2]When the sounds of digraphs vary the whole word has to be perceived in order to know the phonic content of the digraph, e.g., b*ough*, c*ough*, en*ough*, thr*ough* th*ought*, th*ough*.

dyslexic is following with his finger; and if he is distracted from the page he has great difficulty in finding the place again. In the same way that he cannot recall the look of a word, neither has he any mental picture of the layout of the page.

Orientation

It is not only the shape of a letter but the way it faces which is important. It is generally understood that a cup is a cup, whichever way round it is seen: it does not matter whether the handle is on the right, the left, in front or behind, whether the cup is upside-down or not, it is still a cup and recognisable as that. However, if the bulge of a 'd' is on the right of the vertical stroke it becomes a 'b'; a mirrored 'b' becomes a 'p'; likewise 'w' can become 'm', 'u'/'n', 't'/'f', etc. One boy, for instance, sounded out 'm-a-u-t' for 'want'. So not only does the shape itself have to be remembered, but which way round it is determines the sound it makes.

Recognising the dyslexic in class

Teachers often ask what are the typical mistakes and behaviour which dyslexics manifest in class. An attempt has been made here to categorise these in various ages and stages of a dyslexic's life. One may assume that with the right type of treatment the characteristics may not be quite so evident.

Infants

Small children, when learning to read, need to **recognise** letters. At the age of 5 or 6 they often reverse letters and find difficulty in forming the letter-shapes correctly. They cannot always remember the correct sounds for letters. Usually by the age of 7 these problems have been more or less resolved, and the ability to read (and spell) follows without undue stress. With the dyslexic child this does not happen. It has been suggested that this condition is due to a delay in maturation, and many do improve as the years go by. Some, however, do not.

There has been a theory in vogue that teachers should wait for 'reading readiness' in a child. This entails waiting for perceptual abilities, amongst other factors, to develop sufficiently to be capable of recognising word shapes. This attitude accounts for many wasted years at school, with children becoming more and more frustrated and finally developing emotional problems—which are then often thought to be the cause of the reading problem. If a child is not making normal progress at the infant stage, it is vital for it to be recognised that he may have a perceptual problem, and steps should be taken to train him in letter recognition, linking sounds to letters with a view to word-building.

The reading problem is often the first clue that teachers or parents have of a child's dyslexia. The teacher may notice a wide discrepancy between the child's oral ability and his reading ability (and an even wider one between his oral answers and his written ones). Parents may become aware that one of their children is experiencing far more difficulty in reading than his brothers and sisters did. It should always be borne in mind, however, that children do develop at different rates, and merely because one child of the family is slightly behind the rest it does not automatically mean that that child is dyslexic. It must be remembered, too that there is a cluster of disabilities associated with dyslexia. The reading problem is only one aspect of the syndrome.

If an infant has great difficulty in remembering letter-shapes, persistently reversing or rotating[1] some of them, he may need special attention. If he has a problem in relating the correct sounds to letters, in recognising key words or recalling them when he tries to write them, then the teacher should try to work out and apply a remedial programme. After all, this is only finding another way through to that child, and providing a way of teaching by which he may learn. Not all children learn to read in the same way. The whole-word method has proved successful with a majority of pupils, but provision must also be made for the minority. When teaching methods are not geared to a child's particular needs he can often be spotted in class by his restlessness and short span of concentration.

Young Children

By the age of 8 or 9 the dyslexic child is usually slipping further and further behind in reading. Perhaps at 6 years he was only a little behind the average in reading ability for his age, and nobody was particularly worried; but by 8 years he may well have a reading age of 6 years 9 months, and by the age of 10 he may have a reading ability of only 7 years 6 months, representing a $2\frac{1}{2}$-year lag. Should his intelligence be in the 'superior category', however, his reading age should be well above his chronological age—perhaps by as much as two years. So instead of being $2\frac{1}{2}$ years behind in reading age the gap is, in reality, more like $4\frac{1}{2}$ years. No wonder that the intelligent dyslexic child reacts to his failure with feelings of anger and frustration.

For some while he may have managed to hoodwink his teacher. Perhaps he has heard passages in the early readers so often that he knows them by heart. He may get whispered help from a friend, or find some excuse for leaving the classroom when his turn to read is coming up. In the event that he has to read an unfamiliar passage to his teacher, his performance will be full of mis-readings and hesitations. He may yawn frequently and be unable to concentrate. He will perhaps try to divert the teacher's attention to another subject and often becomes adept at introducing red herrings!

His written work will probably be messy, and his handwriting cramped and jagged.[2] His spelling will give many clues to his problem; letters may even at this stage be constantly reversed, and words include incorrectly se-

[1]See *Dyslexia: The Problem of Spelling*, by Joy Pollock, pages 1 and 2.
[2]See *Dyslexia: The Problem of Handwriting*, by Elisabeth Waller.

quenced letters.[1] He may have no idea of where to put a full-stop, what words comprise a sentence, or where to use capital letters. Teachers' remarks at the end of his written work are often: 'Poor spelling'; 'Writing appalling'; and 'Lazy work'. By now he has the reputation of being lazy or stupid, and may well have come to believe this himself. He may withdraw and live in his own dream world; or, he may find that the best way to deal with his predicament is to fool about and take on the role of the class buffoon.

Older Children

Nobody can cope easily with continual failure. Everyone wants to find an area in life in which he can succeed. Ability to succeed gives people confidence in themselves and the urge to take on the challenge of more advanced work. By the age of 11 a dyslexic has probably experienced five or six years of failure in reading and writing at school. His tendency then is to opt out. The more intelligent the child, the more frustrated he is by his own predicament. He may be very much on the defensive; he may have no friends. He does not read for pleasure, and hates reading aloud in class for fear of ridicule. He probably prefers to get his information and entertainment from television rather than books. Despite his intelligence he is often assigned to remedial classes. He will possibly get more and more truculent as the years go by and build up an ever-increasing barrier against learning to read, perhaps saying that reading is unnecessary, and that he can manage without it. Finally, he may join the large number of adult illiterates.

Let us not forget the group of teenagers, mentioned on page 5, who have managed to cope on an average level over the years at school—perhaps in the 'B' or 'C' streams—whereas, according to their intelligence, they should have been amongst the brightest and most academically advanced pupils. They may have a keener sense of failure than children of lower intelligence whose inability to read and spell is more evident, and who therefore get the remedial tuition they require.

Without remedial tuition geared to their particular needs, dyslexics probably fail to get the qualifications necessary for the career of their choice.[2]

[1]See *Dyslexia: The Problem of Spelling*, by Joy Pollock.
[2]Most of them read slowly, but some, mindful of their disability, want to read quickly in order to convince themselves and others that they have overcome their disability. This results in a proliferation of mistakes. They are liable to mis-read examination questions. On the other hand, if they check and re-check their reading of the questions they leave themselves little time for the answers. The fact that they often write slowly and need to give extra attention to syntax and punctuation, apart from spelling, entails yet further problems. It is encouraging that concessions are now being given in public examinations for diagnosed dyslexics.

Some suggestions for dealing with the problem

Once it is understood that a dyslexic's reading problem stems from poor visual perception, poor auditory perception, and difficulties in the sequencing and orientation of letters, the type of remedial tuition needed becomes clearer. Many teachers who are sensitive to their pupils' needs have devised suitable ways of helping them. But when the whole problem of dyslexia is more fully understood, all aspects of the syndrome can be catered for, and then the remedial tuition becomes much more effective. Additionally, the teacher who knows what to do will feel confident of success. The pupil will respond and develop a more positive attitude.

First and foremost the teacher must help to restore the pupil's confidence, whether child or adult. If he has experienced failure in a particular area of learning for some time, he feels vulnerable and tends to sheer away from his difficulty rather than tackle it. It is therefore important that the teacher should explain simply and sympathetically to his pupil what the problem is. He may then be assured that, if he is prepared to work hard and with determination, he can with help be reasonably confident of success. In fact, one often hears of the dyslexic child of a family developing a far stronger character than his siblings, simply because he has had to learn from an early age to come to grips with his problems and get the better of them.

The pupil will probably progress far more quickly in the long run if the teacher devotes the first remedial session to getting to know him—asking him about his family, what he likes and what he dislikes, his hobbies and ambitions, and how he feels about his school. He needs to be warned that although progress may sometimes seem slow every step forward is important and that gradually, but nonetheless surely, he will begin to sort out the muddle and confusion in his mind and get on top of his difficulties. Sometimes pupils arrive for their first lesson hopefully imagining that the teacher will wave some sort of magic wand, and that everything will quickly be alright.

Parents often ask how long their child will need remedial tuition. This is almost impossible to answer as it depends on the severity of the dyslexia, and the child's intelligence. They also often ask if their child will be cured. Rather must they think in terms of overcoming the problem enough for it no longer to be a handicap. Their child's reading might always be slightly faulty and his spelling a little weak, but this need not hold him back. After all there have been a number of eminent people—even professors and authors—with a mild form of this disability.

The main sense involved in reading is that of sight. One sees letters and words, and then perceives their meaning. If a person's perception of symbols is weak, a multi-sensory approach to reading is needed. The senses of hearing and touch are then involved, as well as sight. One then builds on the pupil's strongest area of perception, and trains the weaker areas. If, for instance, his auditory perception is stronger than the visual and kinesthetic, remedial tuition is based on phonics (the **sounds** of letters and digraphs) but training is given in the other areas. In this way reading, writing and spelling are taught together, and not, as is usual, first reading, then spelling. (With the dyslexic it does not automatically follow that the more he reads, the more his spelling improves.) It is generally agreed amongst experienced teachers working with dyslexics that it is necessary to work from the spoken word to word-building, and then to tackle writing and reading. In other words, in learning to spell the dyslexic also learns to read.[1]

Training Visual Perception

Programmes have been devised to improve the child's recognition of shapes and attention to slight differences between drawings of objects, and to see one object or shape in relation to another. The programmes train a child to look carefully, which is a basic essential when learning to read. Other material, not programmed, can also be used for the same purpose. One practice which has met with success is to train the child to look at and discuss pictures, noting details. The following equipment has been found useful:

1) The firm, Learning Development Aids, produce packs of cards for training discrimination in shapes.
2) Frostig Programme for Training in Visual Perception consists of material graded for the beginner, intermediate and advanced levels.
3) *Look* workbooks, by Juliet Reeve and Jean Jackson, provide useful training in perceptual ordering.
4) Fun Books and Play Pads (usually obtainable from any local stationer) devote many pages to differences and similarities of shapes.

Although these offer good initial training in visual perception, it is essen-

---

[1] This has been corroborated by work done both at the Word-Blind Centre in London (which closed in 1971) and at the Word-Blind Institute in Copenhagen, where teaching has been in progress since 1939.

tial to continue the process by teaching the dyslexic to recognise and remember the shapes of letters.

5) The following type of material, where the pupil underlines the letters on the right which are the same as those in the margin, provides training in accurate recognition of letter-shapes:

a	c d a g ɒ o a d
n	u n h m u ∩ n h
c	c ɔ a n c u o a
b	d h b p b g d h
w	m v w u m w v w
my	wy mh my mu my ym
du	bu dn du bn bu du dy
at	at af ta ct at gt at
bed	deb beb bed bad bed
can	acn cau ɔan can nac
big	dig dog big biy gib

Training Auditory Perception

First it is essential to train children to listen carefully and discriminate between sounds.[1]

The following ideas have been found to be helpful:

1) Tape some common sounds, such as a telephone ringing, a match being struck, a car being started up, etc. The pupil can listen to each sound and try to identify it.

2) Rattle an object in a tin. One might first, for instance, take a rubber, then a twopence-piece, then one penny, and a half-penny, after that, perhaps, two or three paper-clips. Not only does a distinctive sound have to be listened for, but the number of objects estimated as well.

3) With a pencil tap a short rhythm (four or five taps to begin with) on the table. The pupil listens carefully and copies the rhythm. If he has difficulty, hold his hand and repeat the rhythm so that he **feels** it, as well as hears it. Let him try again on his own. This training in the rhythm of words, and so of language, is an important part of remedial tuition.

4) Tap or clap the rhythm of a nursery rhyme or popular tune. The pupil should be asked to name it. In this way he becomes aware that language can be conveyed through rhythm alone—as in the case of the African 'talking drums'.

5) Make up a sentence—either short, or longer with clauses, depending on the ability of the pupil. Ask him to repeat it. (It is significant that many dyslexic pupils find accurate repetition difficult. They have poor short term auditory memory.) The game 'I went to market and bought . . .' is a variation on this theme and can be fun to play in a small remedial group.

Discrimination between letter-sounds must follow.

6) From a page of drawn objects ask the pupil to point to all those beginning with 't', then perhaps 'd', and 'p', etc.

7) Place cards of each vowel on the table, and each time the short vowel sound occurs in a word spoken, the pupil should pick out the appropriate letter. If he is confusing the sounds 'e' and 'i', for example, give him the words 'pen', 'pin', 'pig', 'peg', 'pit', 'pet', etc., as practice in discrimination between these two letter-sounds. Finger-puppet vowels provide an amusing version of this for small children.

---

[1] It is often a relief in remedial sessions for children to get away from the background noise which is now so common to everyday living.

8) There are pictures of objects, with their names alongside, but omitting a single letter or digraph which then has to be filled in by the pupil. This is useful material. Care, however, should be taken to provide simple, phonically regular examples in the early stages. Stott Programmed Reading Kit and Tutorpack Phonic and Remedial Reading Programmes are valuable for exercises of this kind.

Tactile and Kinesthetic Training

When both auditory and visual perception are weak, the pupil will learn better through touch and movement. He will find it easier to write a word correctly (or attempt to write it!) than to visualise it or hear its phonic components. He may be more ready to learn through writing, and his spelling will probably be better than his reading, which is the opposite of the normal.

The following are some suggestions for tactile and kinesthetic training. Let the pupil:

1) Make letter shapes with plasticine.
2) Cut letter shapes out of sandpaper, then, with eyes shut, run an index finger over the shape trying to recognise it.
3) Make letter shapes in the air, bringing the whole arm and shoulder muscles into play. This can also be done on the surface of a table.
4) Draw letter shapes, and then short words, on the blackboard, again emphasising the use of the whole arm in the process.
5) Trace over the outline of letters, executing the formation correctly. Reinforce this with the sound of each letter.[1]

Reading disability, therefore, should not be seen as an isolated problem, but rather as part of a larger language problem.[2] For the dyslexic a multisensory training, which includes visual perception and auditory perception, as well as the tactile and kinesthetic, is required.

Three Multi-Sensory Methods

The following techniques incorporate a comprehensive multi-sensory approach to remedial tuition:

1) *The Edith Norrie Letter-Case* is very useful in teaching the early stages of reading. Edith Norrie, who was dyslexic, devised this letter-case

---

[1]See *Dyslexia: The Problem of Spelling,* by Joy Pollock, page 20 (revised edition).
[2]See The Bullock Report *A Language for Life.*

through teaching herself to read and spell.

Pupils are fascinated to see how letter-sounds are made with the mouth. This is seen with the aid of the mirror provided, and the letters are then found in the relevant section in the letter-case. Vowels are in red, and the short vowel sounds are learnt with the help of a Clue Card,[1] which can be made by the pupil. A number of short, phonically regular words is built up, the pupil noting the sound of each letter and whether it is made with the lips, tip-of-the-tongue, or throat. Each letter, however, needs to be given a pure sound so that the pupil can listen to the sounds and hear the word. (mu-a-tu sounds more like 'matter' than 'mat'.)

As each word is finished and correct, it is covered and the pupil asked to recall the shape and letter-content. He is asked to try and picture the number of letters in a particular word, whether there is a red letter (vowel), whether there are more letters before or after the red letter, whether there is a tall letter, and if so, where it comes in the word, etc. This training in visual recall in turn aids recognition of words, which is what reading is.

Gradually he progresses to four- and five-letter, and then multisyllabic words. Digraphs and certain letter combinations, such as 'tion' can be practised. This gives clues to words when reading in context, and later increases the speed of reading.

Blending sounds aloud trains a left-to-right attack on words. This develops later into scanning silently and, finally, to whole-word recognition. This process will be reinforced by writing.

This method gives both children and adults the key to the decoding of totally new words.

Punctuation is also included in the letter-case. Punctuation symbols are important for dyslexics, who usually find their use particularly difficult. Without an awareness of the conventional use of full-stops, commas, etc., they are unlikely to understand what they read.

2) *The Pictogram System* offers another multi-sensory approach to reading, designed with the dyslexic in mind. Each letter is represented by a character, either human or animal, so drawn as to emphasise the **shape** of the letter. This aids in the recall of the sound that goes with it. There is Ticking Tom, for instance, which is a ✦ looking like a telegraph pole. He keeps ticking and saying 't-t-t'. Then there are the 'kicking king' and the 'hairy hat-man' and many others, including 'robber red' and his band. These robbers capture vowels, either silencing them, or changing their sounds while in the band's power, so

[1]See *Dyslexia: The Problem of Spelling*, by Joy Pollock.

18

producing the murmuring vowels ar, or, and er, ir, and ur.

The stories about each letter have the imagination which appeals to children, and indeed the initial inspiration came from children in remedial classes. Practically all the characters face to the right, subtly reinforcing the left-to-right attack of the reading process.

The tales about the relationships of one letter to another introduces digraphs and letter-combinations. There are, for instance, the 'Boot and Foot twins' who fight over their boots; there is the 'clever cat' who sneezes when he comes beside the 'hairy hat-man', saying 'ch'. The visual stimulus of the picture-code, and the stories which reinforce the phonic content of the letter symbols, provide interesting training in both visual and auditory perception for the younger pupil.

3) *The Gillingham-Stillman Method* has much to offer teachers who prefer their remedial teaching to follow a formal routine. This method is based on linking the relevant letter-combinations of phonemes and digraphs to the appropriate sound. The pupil learns by rote all the possible ways of representing a particular sound for spelling. He is trained in phonic drill so that he will be able to apply the sounds for reading. At the end of each session he is given a dictation which includes only those letter-sounds which have been learnt. He is never expected to read or write anything which has not already been taught in the remedial sessions. In this way he acquires confidence through success.

Most of the basic spelling rules and guides, which teachers should know, are incorporated into this system. For instance, all, full and till drop an 'l' when added to another word or syllable; 'f', 'l' and 's' are doubled after a short vowel at the end of a monosyllabic word.

This method also accentuates multi-sensory training, using exercises and games to develop and reinforce the student's auditory, visual, kinesthetic and vocal abilities in connection with language training.

As with the Edith Norrie Letter-Case, the phonogram cards take a pupil through the process of gradually building up words of increasing complexity and length, giving him insight into the structure of words.

Some modifications of the Gillingham-Stillman Method are also being used in clinics and remedial centres.

These three schemes provide structured and systematic language training. They may be used alongside each other, the one reinforcing the other, depending on the needs of the pupil. The Edith Norrie Letter-Case is a particularly flexible piece of equipment.

In order to aid 'a teacher using a systematic, structured approach to language' Gill Cotterell has produced a *Box of Phonic Reference Cards.* These, and the accompanying *Check List of Basic Sounds,* are an invaluable aid for the teacher of the older intelligent student. Basic spelling rules and guides are incorporated. Prefixes and suffixes, with information about their derivations, are provided. This enables pupils to break words up into prefixes, stems and suffixes, and study the parts, before synthesising them into the whole word.

This is important training for the dyslexic, who finds it difficult to see where one syllable ends and the next begins. Study of word derivations helps him to deduce the meaning of unfamiliar words, and consequently to improve his comprehension of passages of text.

Some further suggestions

The Complete Beginner

If a pupil knows no letters at all, begin with the first letter of his name as this has particular significance for him. In practice, however, most pupils know at least a few letters when they begin their remedial tuition. Practically all of them can write their Christian names, and this provides a remedial teacher with a few letters with which to begin.

Let us suppose a child is called Justin. Ask him to write his name in large letters on a sheet of paper, giving him guidance over the execution of the shapes where necessary. Cut out the letters. Place the six pieces on the table and, giving the sounds for each letter in turn, ask the child to find them. Then ask him to give the sounds when he is shown the letters one by one. Now there are at least a few letters where he recognises both the shapes and the sounds. This is a starting point. Short phonically regular words can be made up from these letters—in, sun, tin, nut, sit, jut, just, tins, nuts. Gradually more letters are added—perhaps the letters of his surname, or of the names of brothers and sisters. The letters that he knows are kept in an envelope with his name on. These are his own special letters which he adds to lesson by lesson, building up an increasing number of words. Drawing pictures and writing the words alongside will help him to become more familiar with these letters and aid in their recognition.

Where names are not phonically regular the digraph should be introduced later. Lyn Wendon, in her Pictogram System, recommends that the phonetically irregular letters have a square put round them to help the child remember that these letters make a special sound, and will be learnt in due course.

Any of the three multi-sensory methods mentioned above may be introduced at this stage.

Children with Short Span of Concentration

Lack of concentration may only affect certain activities. A child who will not (or cannot!) sit still with a book may spend hours playing with airfix models or painting pictures. A situation needs to be created in which he can develop this same concentration in reading. Some children feel so inhibited by books at the time they come for their remedial tuition that a teacher must devise all sorts of pre-reading and reading activities. An observant teacher will be able to tell whether the pupil who talks incessantly throughout the lesson is needing to unload some of his anxieties and should be listened to with patience, or is creating a diversion in order to maintain the barrier that he has set up between himself and the business of reading. In the latter case he will need to be given the confidence to dare to try yet again to master something at which he has been failing for years. In a session of three-quarters of an hour as many as twelve to fifteen different approaches might have to be used to hold these children's attention. The following are some suggestions:

1) Listening games.
2) Tapping or clapping rhythms.
3) Matching objects, letters, or words. This can also be played as a game of Pairs.
4) Classifying objects, or words.
5) Selecting, for instance, all the 'd's from a pile of random letters.
6) Playing 'I Spy', giving the letter-sounds (not names).
7) Blending games, such as 'g-oa-t', what is it?
8) Rhyming games, such as 'cat', give me a word that rhymes with it?
9) Simple word-building, with, perhaps, the child's collection of known letters.
10) Using apparatus from the Stott Programmed Reading Kit.
11) Seeing, with the use of a mirror, how letter-sounds are made in the mouth, and relating these to letter-shapes.
12) Working through a programme on the Tutorpack.
13) Tracking (a method of improving scanning and learning the order of letters in the alphabet).
14) Using Learning Development Aid Cards, for training visual recall, etc.
15) Using Fun Books or Play Pads, for observing similarities, differences.
16) Playing Kim's Game, using objects which the child can spell.
17) Writing letter-shapes on the blackboard, and after some practice then doing it blindfold.
18) Playing Phonic Rummy, or Phonic Sets.
19) Sequencing days, months, seasons.
20) Learning to tell the time, the points of the compass, right and left.
21) Learning to tie shoe laces, ties, bows (sequence of actions).
22) Playing games, such as, 'I went to market and bought . . .' and 'I had a birthday and got . . .'.
23) Talking to the child and encouraging him to express himself verbally.
24) Asking the child to describe an incident or story, perhaps on a tape recorder.
25) Reading a story to the child.

Within the allotted time there should always be included as much reading and writing as possible, but the child should **never** be pressurised.

Remedial Teaching in Groups

Remedial groups are not only an advantage for economic reasons, but also an advantage for the child who feels alone with his failure. It is here that he meets others with problems similar to his own, and gains courage and hope through sharing experiences.

Three pupils in a group for an hour's tuition allows a teacher the opportunity to give each some individual help, as well as working with the group as a whole. In every lesson the aim should be to incorporate training in the following:

1) Auditory perception—recognition of sounds, and phonics.
2) Visual perception—recognition and recall of shapes, letters, and words.
3) Reading, including meanings of words and comprehension of text.
4) Writing, including spelling, handwriting, word analysis and some word derivation.
5) Sequencing and Orientation.

A teacher will be helped in her objective if she provides apparatus which enables the pupil to correct his own work. This has the added advantage that the child is encouraged to improve on his own previous standard, rather than compete with the others. Children are often in a competitive atmosphere in class, where dyslexics suffer a sense of failure. It is important that these attitudes should not be carried over into a remedial group. Much of the Stott Programmed Reading Kit is self-correcting, and also the programmes of the Tutorpack Teaching Machine.

With two children working on programmed material, a teacher is freed to give individual attention to the third pupil.

It is essential that a teacher keeps notes of each pupil's progress, and records of the types of mistakes made. Rectifying these forms the basis of further tuition. Elimination of mistakes is a very gradual process, so there needs to be continual reinforcement of spelling guides already learnt.

Many a child in a remedial group has been helped over his embarrassment at reading aloud in front of others when he has realised that they, too, are in a similar predicament. If he can learn as well to laugh at his own mistakes in reading, he will be less vulnerable to ridicule in class.

Remedial groups offer an ideal opportunity to play the games listed on page 22—perhaps in the last five or ten minutes of the lesson.

A check should be made that every dyslexic knows, in their correct order, the days of the week, the months and seasons, as well as being able to read and spell them. The alphabet, telling the time, looking up words in dictionaries, the points of the compass, and right and left should also be included in remedial sessions.

The Adult Dyslexic

Recent statistics have shown that there are at least two million 'functional illiterates' in the United Kingdom. Experts working on research into dyslexia have found that the incidence is much higher than was first indicated. It can safely be assumed that many of these illiterates are, in fact, dyslexic.

It is particularly important that adult dyslexics should not be allowed to feel humiliated by coming for remedial lessons. It takes a lot of courage for a grown person to acknowledge that he needs tuition in literacy. However, all of us could benefit from remedial training in some area of our lives. If a teacher bears in mind that an adult dyslexic could probably teach him something of use as well, an atmosphere of mutual respect will be generated.

Any apparatus or books that are reminiscent of the early years at school and of past failures should be avoided. This creates difficulties over the selection of reading matter as there is little available for an adult with a very low reading age. Initial stages in reading may be built up round words with which he comes into daily contact—'open', 'closed' and 'shut'; 'on' and 'off'; road signs and names of pubs; his address and the names of his family. Learning the names of local stations on his way to and from work will enable him to get about more confidently. (One adult arrived very late for an appointment because, at each station on the underground, he had had to get out and compare the name of the station on his piece of paper with the one on the platform.)

Having learnt a word like 'stop', he can then go on to other short phonically regular words that end with '-op', and to those which begin with 'st'; then the short vowel sounds can be changed, 'step', then 'tip', 'top', 'tap', etc. In this way the pupil begins to see some regularity in words. He then feels more confident about tackling them on his own. The 'phonic key' unlocks the door to reading.

As time goes on, the emphasis in a lesson should be varied according to the interests and employment of the pupil. A plumber, for instance, will need to read and write the vocabulary of his trade; an actor may need to improve his reading so that he can cope with auditions more confidently. One pupil may feel that learning to fill in a form or worksheet is of high priority. Another, finding letter-writing a source of much embarrassment, may wish for guidance in layout and form. Examples of various types of letters—answering an invitation, applying for a job, etc.—will provide a useful basis on which he can plan his own.

A sensitive approach on the part of the teacher is essential. Adults with severe reading disabilities tend to feel alone with their problem. If, during a lesson, a teacher can weave in information about others who have reached maturity unable to read, tell the time, sequence the months (or whatever is appropriate) much comfort and reassurance will be gained by the pupil. This is often followed by his determination to master the problem.

The Intelligent Teenager

For those intelligent teenagers in need of remedial tuition to get through examinations necessary for higher education, there should be a different approach from that required for the illiterate adult. They, too, however, must not be allowed to feel humiliated by coming for remedial tuition. Offering a 'course in linguistics' may help to allay any fears of childish treatment. With years of under-achievement behind them, they are usually convinced that they are stupid, and they probably feel apprehensive about trying to get professional qualifications. Where justified, much reassurance needs to be given.

At this stage in their academic lives they are using a vocabulary geared to the subjects in which they are specialising. Rectifying faulty reading and mis-spellings of words with which they are having difficulty will enable them to feel more confident about the use of terminology they have to cope with daily. Realisation of improvement gives hope of succeeding.

Word analysis, including study of prefixes[1] and suffixes, trains a dyslexic to see which letters are usually grouped together. Improvement in reading ability follows and, later, increased speed. Work on word derivation enables him to understand more about the structure of words, and improves comprehension. With the Edith Norrie Letter-Case and the Phonic Reference Cards a teacher is able to build up structured remedial training to meet the needs of the pupil. This improves both reading and spelling.

In the case of a very slow reader cassette tapes can be helpful. If the dyslexic can find someone to record the important passages of text, if not a whole book, this will save him much time and relieve him of much pressure. Time is often a vital factor in a dyslexic's academic life as the process of reading and writing may take much longer than it does for other pupils. (Some students have been known to take carbon copies of their notes to help a dyslexic friend.) Courses on tapes are now being produced commercially, and these may be invaluable for the slow reader.

It is particularly helpful for a dyslexic if he is shown how to get the 'meat' from a text book—first studying the chapter headings, then reading the introduction, dipping into the middle, and finally carefully reading the conclusion.

[1]Dictionaries, such as *Webster's Dictionary* and *Highroad's Dictionary*, published by Nelson, give the meanings of prefixes.

Conclusion

Learning to read is a complicated process. People are complex individuals. When **people** are involved with **reading** the variations in learning are innumerable. As stated in the Bullock Report *A Language for Life* there is no one way of teaching reading. For dyslexics, however, there should be individual variations on a multi-sensory approach.

Any written information on teaching techniques tends to sound dogmatic. Teachers need to digest ideas and apply what is appropriate. Reading Tests, too, should be used with discretion. It is the way the test is done and the types of mistakes made that are of value to the remedial teacher, rather than the reading age obtained. (The latter, in any case, varies from one test to another.) On the basis of the information gained a teacher learns how best to help the pupil.

The onus is on the teacher to create a situation in which the pupil feels he can tackle successfully any reading or word-building given. Dyslexics initially learn to read through learning to word-build or spell. In the early stages there will be many lessons without any reading books at all.

Reading is more than accurate decoding of written symbols. It is communication of ideas through these symbols. When a person can read there is a wealth of information—both literary and instructive—at his disposal. Without this skill people are deprived of a basic tool of modern life. Many of them withdraw or become delinquent. The time is now ripe, indeed overdue, for educationalists to re-assess their views on the teaching of reading.

One highly intelligent dyslexic who had built up his own business with great success, even though he could barely read the letters he dictated to his secretary, had this to say: "I know I'm intelligent, and my I.Q. test confirmed this. It's not my fault that I didn't learn to read at school. They just did not understand my problem." As teachers, let us ensure that we do understand, and that **every** child learns to read.